Squash Rules O.K.

Squash Rules O.K.

JOHN TIMPERLEY
Foreword by Geoff Hunt

Published by EP Publishing Limited, Bradford Road, East Ardsley, West Yorkshire, WF3 2JN

© John Timperley 1983

ISBN 0 7158 0874 5 (cased)
      0 7158 0875 3 (limp)

British Library Cataloguing in Publication Data

Timperley, John
    Squash rules O.K.
    1. Squash rackets (Game) — Rules
    I. Title
    796.34'3'0202   GV1004

    ISBN 0-7158-0875-3

Printed and bound in Italy by
Legatoria Editoriale Giovanni Olivotto, Vicenza.

Typesetting and design by
The Word Factory, Rossendale, Lancashire.

Contents

Foreword

John Timperley's knowledge of the rules, his vast experience as a marker and referee, and his active sense of humour have resulted in this exacting and amusing study of the rules of squash.

I recommend the book to players, to referees and markers, and to spectators. I found it easy to understand and very enjoyable.

Geoff Hunt

About the author

John Timperley is a self-confessed squash nut.

At an age approaching senility, after playing for England at badminton, he adopted squash as his main sporting activity — with notable success.

He played squash at county level and qualified as an advanced amateur coach. As an international referee he served on the referees' and markers' committee of the Squash Rackets Association and is now a highly respected and widely travelled tournament administrator. In his written works and his television commentaries there is a simple message — squash should be fun. This book will help others achieve that objective.

The artists

Hugh Silvey and Wally Jex have never played squash, but their illustrations capture the maniacal aspects of two people being locked in a room, knocking hell out of a little rubber ball.

As illustrators, the Silvey-Jex partnership has contributed to the success of many well-known television advertising campaigns. They also write and illustrate their own books.

Introduction

'If you don't enjoy it, you shouldn't do it!' This maxim applies as much to squash as it does to marathon running, climbing Everest or deep-sea diving.

Think about it. Think about the last time you failed to enjoy a game of squash. Chances are that you or your opponent failed to agree on a simple matter of principle. Or, to put it another way, one of you didn't know the rules.

This book is about the rules of squash as they should be interpreted by fair-minded, consenting people. Knowing them will help you towards a greater enjoyment of all your games, and will also extend your squash friendships.

That way you'll be able to concentrate on the real objective — to devastate your opponents, rather than give them an excuse for losing!

Who's running the show?

On the way to your personal pinnacle of squash success you'll occasionally find yourself under the control of two officially appointed custodians of justice— the Marker and the Referee. Sometimes one person will perform both roles, but ideally the pair should be present to attend to their separate tasks.

The functions of these two officials are important, so it will pay you to understand why they are invited along, at enormous expense, to try and ruin the game for you.

The first thing you'll notice is that neither of them is quite as useless as he may look. By using score sheets to record the players' names and, when the match begins, to mark down the score, they write the story of the match.

The Marker does most of the talking and likes the sound of his own voice. He's the noisy blighter who calls the score and conducts the match. For example, during the knock-up he'll tell the players when they've had half-time, and he'll also tell them when it's time to start the match.

During an actual game the Marker will use very precise, universally adopted terminology to advise the players when one of them has served a fault, hit the ball out of court, or generally failed to keep a rally going properly.

In effect, when a Marker makes a call during a match he is expressing an opinion about the validity of a particular shot. In a well-conducted match, the two players and the Marker can solve most of the problems without anybody else's help.

However, if a player disagrees with the Marker's reading of the match, or if he considers the score has been incorrectly called, he can lodge an appeal to the other official, the Referee, by saying, 'May I appeal about...'

The Referee is the strong, silent type, who needs waking up now and then to deal with this sort of problem— which may occur at any moment during the match. He has overall control, can agree or disagree with the player's viewpoint and will award lets or strokes to players who have been disadvantaged.

There may be times when a player is impeded during a rally and play breaks down. He will feel that he would like the rally to be played again. If this is the case, the offended player can make an appeal to the Referee, by using the words 'Let, please' as his opening gambit.

In making such a discreet and courteous appeal, a player is doing all that he can under the rules, though in many instances the Referee can, and will, award a stroke to one of the players without having the rally played again.

Sweetness and light are the keys to successful appeals in squash. Be polite. It will be to your advantage if the Referee reaches the conclusion that you are a fair-minded individual, and it will help him make fair-minded decisions.

So there it is. The Marker assumes verbal control of the match until problems arise. Then the Referee takes over and gets the match going again. Any decision made by the Referee will be repeated by the Marker before he announces the score and play continues.

The Referee is a pretty powerful bloke and he is trying to do a difficult job well. So make him your friend and treat him with respect. If you're 7–8 down in the fifth game, you might need him to exercise the judgement of Solomon in your favour!

Rough or smooth?

Whether you've got an official Marker and Referee, one person doing both jobs, or no one at all, always try to conduct yourself as though the officials were there. That way you'll be getting yourself ready for the big events, and in the meantime you'll command the respect of your opponents.

Here are a few pointers to get you into battle without aggravation:

- **Don't be late.** If you turn up for a match more than ten minutes later than the scheduled time you risk disqualification. It's a very tiresome way to lose a match.

- **During your match make sure that there are only five
  items on court — two players, two rackets, and a
  ball.** All the accompanying paraphernalia, like towels,
  spare rackets, suitcases and other bric-à-brac items
  should be removed. This is a game of squash — not a
  jumble sale.

- **Unless you've got special dispensation from a
  competition organizer, it is recommended that you
  wear clothing which is white, and/or of a 'light
  matching pastel' colour.** One day, if you're playing in
  front of the television cameras you might be asked to
  wear coloured clothing and advertising slogans,
  but until that time, try to be a vestal virgin. If you look
  good, you'll feel good!

● **Have you closed the door properly?**

Good. Now you can start the five minute knock-up.

Use the knock-up intelligently. It's not a rule, but a matter of common courtesy that players should have an equal opportunity to practise their shots. So, get your stroking going and give your opponent the same chance.

After two and a half minutes the Marker will announce that you've had half-time and that you can change positions with your opponent to allow you to practise shots on the other side of the court. Contrary to popular belief, it is not compulsory that you change sides, and Markers who *instruct* players to change sides are exceeding their authority.

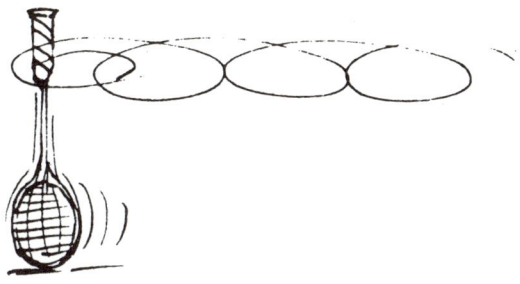

However, if the Marker does tell you to change sides, stay cool — you've got bigger problems to solve than that and it's much too early in the match to be falling out with the officials.

You'll know that your moment of truth has arrived when the Marker calls out the word 'time'. It's one of those precise and universally adopted squash words which means that it's time for the match to begin in earnest.

So spin your racket, and get going.

The match will be awarded to the first player to win three games. In other words, you are playing the best of five games and at the conclusion of the match, one of the players will have won by either 3–0, 3–1, or 3–2.

The first player to score nine points wins a game, but there is one exception. When the score reaches 8–8 in a game for the first time, the receiver can decide to extend the game so that it will be won by whoever scores ten points first. Alternatively, if the receiver declines to extend the game, it is won by the person whose score first reaches nine points.

The receiver's decision must be clearly indicated to his opponent and to the officials. Usually, of course, he will 'set' the game to finish at ten points (called *set two*) to guard against losing the next rally unluckily.

Sometimes the receiver will announce his decision with a seemingly impolite gesture of the hand. There are a limited number of occasions when you can use the 'two-fingered' gesture and get away with it, but this is one of them. And you can do it without even opening your mouth!

The alternative decision on the part of the receiver (called *no set*) is quite acceptable — especially if you're a cool unflappable type of person, who can handle yourself in a shoot-out.

The service

Very few squash players take sufficient care to serve the ball properly, which is ironic, because if you've won the right to serve, you can win the next rally and add a point to your score. Even if you're losing your match 0–9, 0–9, 0–8, this is true. You can still win!

Never waste an opportunity to serve well, because it will maximize your chance of scoring points and winning games.

The first thing to remember, after you've won the right to serve, is that you can choose whether to serve from the forehand or the backhand side of the court. Most people serve to their opponent's backhand on the first occasion, though you do have the choice and you can start from either side.

Thereafter, as long as you retain the right to serve, you must alternate between the two sides.

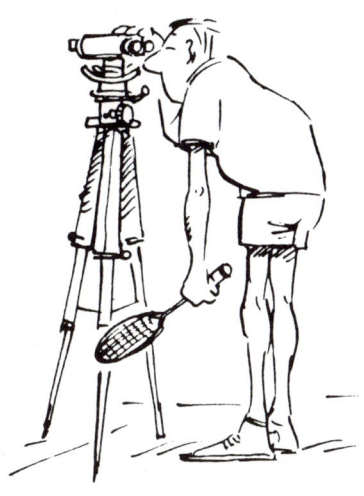

To serve legally you should do the following:

- **Stand with at least one foot on the floor, inside the service box.**

- **Throw, or drop, the ball into the air.**

- **Hit the ball with the racket onto the front wall, above the middle red line.**

- **Ensure that the first bounce of the ball on the floor (if it isn't volleyed) is in the back quarter of the court, on the side opposite you, the server.**

It really is quite straightforward.

The next thing to remember about serving is that you have three simple options:

- **You can serve legally and well and, by winning the rally, place yourself in the happy position of being able to add a point to your score.**

- **You can either serve a fault or make a foot-fault and so put yourself at a minor, temporary disadvantage.**

- **You can commit 'temporary suicide' by serving your hand out.**

Let's take these last two points one at a time.

Serving a fault

Serving a fault isn't a capital offence because you get another chance. However, if you do serve a fault, you usually give your opponent an advantage he hasn't earned. He can play the fault service, or leave it, whichever suits him best — and he doesn't have to tell you which option he selects. All he has to do is to play the ball if he thinks it would benefit him. If he decides to leave it you have one more opportunity to serve.

Fault services are created in the following ways:

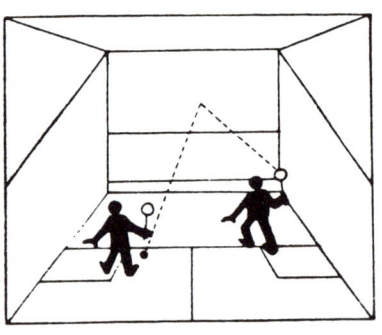

- **Hitting the ball without having one foot on the floor, completely inside the appropriate service box.**

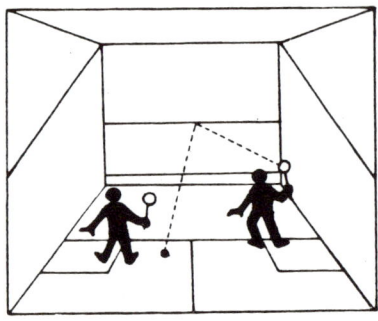

- **Serving the ball onto or below the middle line on the front wall.**

With every one of these fault services, assuming your opponent has not attempted to play the ball, you are allowed one more turn to serve properly. If you fail to do so at the next attempt you will have 'served your hand out', and the right to serve passes to your opponent.

But don't worry if your first service is a combination of more than one fault. It only counts as one, and you can have another try.

- **Serving the ball so that, after hitting the front wall, it bounces on, or in front of, the line across the floor of the court.**

- **Serving the ball into the incorrect quarter court. In other words, hitting it back to yourself, and not across the court into the opposite quarter.**

Serving hand out

It's an unusual phrase, 'serving hand out', but it's worth remembering because it describes an important aspect of playing squash — the act of committing temporary suicide. This means you lose the right to continue serving because of a serious error in your delivery of the service. It can happen in a number of ways, such as by:

- **Hitting the ball out of court after striking the front wall.**

- **Hitting the ball onto the board (or tin) at the bottom of the front wall.**

- **Hitting the ball onto any part of the court — for example a side wall — before hitting the front wall.**

- **Allowing the ball to strike a wall or the floor before being hit.**

    In other words, you must not allow the ball to bounce on the floor or the wall prior to hitting it. It must be dropped from your hand, or if first thrown in the air it must be allowed to fall, directly onto the racket.

- **Failing to strike the ball after it has been thrown in the air, or dropped.**

- **Striking the ball more than once in the act of serving.**

- **Serving two consecutive faults.**

    This is an interesting aspect of squash rules. You do not serve 'double faults'. If you serve two faults consecutively you are considered to have 'served your hand out', just as you would have done if you had hit the service out of court.

Receiving service

As the receiver, it is important that you familiarize yourself with the option available to you if your opponent serves a fault.

It is a choice which is open only to the receiver — the server has none — so make sure of your general strategy before you play.

If you are the receiver and your opponent serves a fault you can take it or leave it. Simply that. Take it . . . or leave it.

If you decide to play the fault-service the fault is forgiven and forgotten, even if, following a breakdown in play, a let is allowed and the point is played again.

Servers who have their faults forgiven and forgotten should be grateful. In squash, forgiveness is rare.

If you are the receiver and you exercise your other choice, which is to leave the fault-service without playing it, the server gets another chance to deliver a good service.

If he serves another, consecutive fault, there are no options available to anyone. Whether you hit the ball or not, he has 'served his hand out' and you become the server.

Very occasionally, a let will be necessary when play breaks down during the rally associated with a *second* service. The point will be played again.

In this event, the fault associated with the original service is not forgiven and forgotten and if the server delivers another fault, he will automatically have 'served his hand out'.

Lets

A let is an undecided stroke, usually resulting from a breakdown in play.

In playing a let, the intention is to put the players back on an even footing so that they have an equal chance, subject to their differing abilities, to win the replayed rally.

In most circumstances the rules require a player to appeal to the Referee if he requires a let, but because most friendly matches are played without a Referee, it is preferable for both players to know their entitlements — and their obligations.

Lets are only allowed if, during the appropriate rally, a player could have made a good return of the ball. It's pretty obvious, but if you are not in a position to get to the ball and strike it, the rules on lets are irrelevant.

So, here's a point to remember: if interference occurs and you intend to ask for a let, move yourself to the scene of the action to show your opponent or the Referee that you could have played the ball. In this way, when you ask for a let, you will be more likely to get one.

There are circumstances when lets *may* be allowed and there are other circumstances when lets *shall* be allowed. We'll separate the two groups and examine them in detail.

Lets may be allowed

The usual situations where you may be entitled to a let are:

- **When you are touched by the ball after playing it, because of the position of your opponent.**

This covers the possibility that your opponent might be blocking your exit from the hitting area, but you must be seen to be making every effort to get out of his way. If you are, there is a good chance you'll get the let.

- **When your opponent shapes up to play one shot and then changes his mind and plays another, leaving you in the path of the ball.**

He is quite entitled to change his mind— he can do it as often as he likes provided he strikes the ball before the second bounce— but equally, you can't be expected to be a mind reader. You are not penalized for placing yourself in the correct position for him to play his first shot, but in the wrong position for the shot which he attempts to play after changing his mind. You may be entitled to a let.

- **When the ball touches any article lying in the court.**

For this purpose, a prostrate player is not deemed to be an 'article lying in the court'.

- **When you refrain from playing the ball because of a reasonable fear of injuring your opponent.**

This is another obvious rule. Most squash players are intelligent, reasonable, sensible people. That's why they play squash in the first place — so there won't be too many arguments about requesting a let for fear of causing injury. Everyone knows it makes sense.

- **When, in the act of playing the ball, you touch your opponent — either with your racket or with some part of your person.**

Normally, if you play the ball after being impeded you are reckoned to have accepted any disadvantage caused by the interference, and the rally will continue. But if you suffer interference in the actual execution of the shot, and that interference places you at a disadvantage, you can discontinue the rally and claim a let.

If the Referee is still awake and agrees that interference did occur, he will allow a let. However, don't forget — the law is not concerned with trifles. Lets can be refused, so keep the rally going unless you are really inconvenienced.

- **When the Referee is asked to decide an appeal and is unable to do so.**

Squash cynics have been known to suggest that this section in the rules is the salvation of sleepy Referees because it enables them to maintain their credibility when they doze off in the gallery. But seriously, there are occasions when a Referee, for a variety of reasons, is unable to make a decision. Usually it's because he's unsighted. If so, he'll probably ask the players to start the rally again. It isn't always the fairest solution but at least it's an attempt to be fair.

- **When a player loses a stroke because his opponent drops a racket, calls out, or causes a distraction in some other way.**

Some people would argue that this rule isn't strong enough to discourage serious and persistent distraction from one of the players. They maintain that a player should suffer a more serious penalty for repeatedly causing distraction, rather than being given another chance to win the rally.

Before we leave this section dealing with the situations when lets may be allowed, we ought to consider, and resolve, the question which baffles many club players, 'Should I call out "turning" if I decide to turn on the ball before playing it?' The answer is emphatically, 'No!'

Any noise, be it a shout, call, grunt or groan, is a form of distraction which should be discouraged, whether you're intending to be polite or not.

Lets shall be allowed

Now we can move on to the section in the rules which says a let shall be allowed. In other words, there is no discretion in the matter.

A let shall be allowed:

- **When the receiver of a service is not ready to accept it and, as a result, he declines to play the ball.**

Obviously, in these circumstances, the server should not be allowed to dash from side to side of the court giving the receiver the bum's rush, but on the other hand, the receiver should not employ delaying tactics to recover his composure or disturb the reasonable momentum of the server in any way.

If you're playing in a competition and you've got an efficient Marker, his calling of the score will give a very good guide to the tempo of events. If that doesn't work, the Referee will award lets where appropriate.

- **When the ball breaks in play.**

   Very occasionally, when a rally ends without incident and the server starts banging the ball about prior to making his next service delivery, the ball will break — but not during play!

   Intense arguments can accompany such incidents, so make the decision now that you will always assume the ball broke during play. Then you can play a let — and save yourself a lot of hassle.

- **When the ball hits a player after his opponent has struck at it, but missed.**

It is a precondition of a let being granted that the ball, after being missed, could have been properly returned if it had not hit the other player. If this isn't the case, a stroke is awarded to the person who was struck by the ball.

Makes you think, doesn't it?

- **When a player misses the ball, recovers, and then strikes his opponent with the ball on its way to the front wall, directly or indirectly.**

We'll cover the more general provisions under which players are struck by the ball later on. The awarding of a let in this situation is only related to a player making a permissible, further attempt to hit the ball after missing it.

Where lets are concerned there is plenty to think about. The most sensible thing to do is to avoid causing them.

The next two sections — the most important in the book — will tell you how.

'Fair view, freedom to play the ball, and interference'

If you took up squash knowing no more than the provisions of the rule entitled 'Fair view, freedom to play the ball, and interference' you could still have an enjoyable game. It is the essence of squash. It is the squash player's eleventh commandment.

That's why you should study it — slowly and deliberately — to ensure that you really understand it and recognize it as the golden key to enjoyable squash.

Look at the exact wording of the first part of this rule: 'After playing a ball, a player must make every effort to get out of his opponent's way.'

That's very simple and easy to understand. 'After playing a ball' means that an instruction is being given to *one* of the players — not both. The player who has just struck the ball, as opposed to the player who is *about* to strike it, is being requested to do all he can to get out of his opponent's way.

So, after you've hit the ball, your feet must take you away from the scene of the action. You must make every effort to do so. Not just an effort to do so. *Every effort.* Nothing less will do. Goodbye. Push off and go to another part of the court.

In the next section of the rule the phrase 'must make every effort' is repeated three times in relation to interference. This emphasizes that if you have just struck the ball you must allow your opponent:
a) to see the ball,
b) to play it freely without hindrance, and
c) to hit it directly to the front wall or to the side walls near the front wall.

And if you don't and interference occurs? The rule says this: 'If . . . in the opinion of the Referee, the player has not made every effort . . . the Referee . . . shall . . . award the stroke to his opponent.'

Isn't that brutally clear? If you don't make the required effort, you've got no chance of winning the rally. You're dead. Kaput. You lose the stroke.

So in future, before you tuck yourself in for the night, keep repeating the squash player's eleventh commandment, 'After playing a ball, I must make every effort to get out of my opponent's way'.

More 'Fair view, freedom to play the ball, and interference'

We now know that if, after playing the ball, you haven't made every effort to get out of your opponent's way, you should automatically lose the stroke.

But what happens when interference occurs and you have made every effort to avoid causing it? The answer is simple. The rule says, in effect, that if you made every effort to avoid causing interference, a let shall be allowed.

Is that clear? If you do make every effort, you play the point again and you get another chance to win the rally.

But don't go away. It isn't quite that simple, because there are three important exceptions to consider:

- **The Referee will award a stroke against a player who has made every effort to get out of his opponent's way if, as a result of the interference, his opponent has been prevented from making a winning return.**

What is a winning return? A multitude of variables will affect the Referee's thinking when he considers whether to award a stroke.

These include:
a) the position of both players on the court,
b) the ability of the players to hit winners in ordinary circumstances,
c) the speed or mobility of the players,
d) the degree of exhaustion of the players, and
e) the pace of the ball.

These are the circumstances, in important matches, when Referees earn their corn. It isn't always easy.

As far as your friendly matches are concerned, if you haven't got a Referee, play a let unless you are both absolutely certain that a stroke would be more appropriate. Stay friends.

The second exception where a Referee will award a stroke against a player who has made every effort to get out of his opponent's way is the subject of widespread misinterpretation amongst players and spectators at every level. In crowded galleries, competent Referees have been reduced to quivering wrecks after making correct, well-reasoned decisions under this second exception because uninformed players or spectators have failed to understand the reasoning behind the decision.

If the rule is that important and contentious, let's go through it with care.

- **When... a player refrains from playing the ball which, if played, would clearly and undoubtedly have won the rally under the terms of Rule 9** [entitled 'Hitting an opponent with the ball']... **he shall be awarded the stroke.**

So what this rule is saying is that when a player refrains from playing a ball, which would, if played, have gone directly to the front wall, he shall be awarded the stroke.

Can you see the point? If the player had hit the ball directly towards the front wall, and hit his opponent with it, he would have won the stroke under the provisions of the rule entitled 'Hitting an opponent with the ball'. Clearly, he should not be worse off if he refrains from playing the ball for fear of hitting his opponent.

There is an additional benefit if a player refrains from playing a ball in these circumstances. He avoids the risk of seriously injuring his opponent.

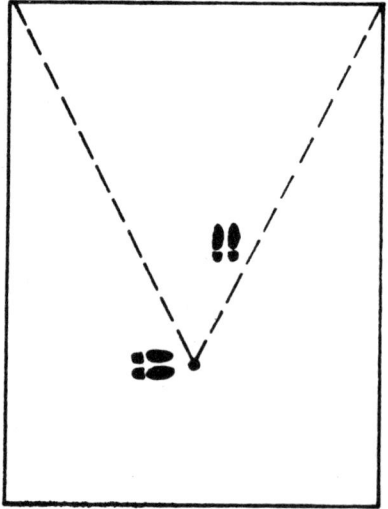 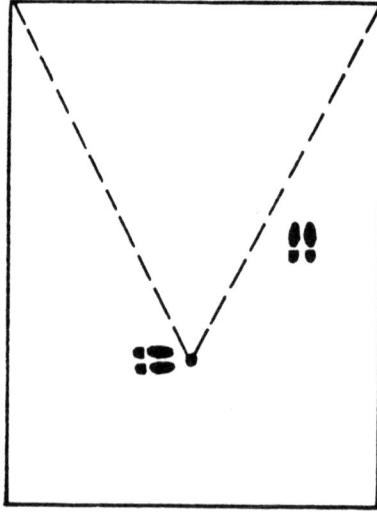

These diagrams show that if it's your turn to play the ball, your opponent should endeavour, in his own interests, to be outside the triangle represented by the front wall and the two extreme lines of the ball's potential flight path. If he's in the triangle, it automatically follows that you *could* hit him with the ball on its way to the front wall.

It is the Referee's responsibility to decide whether the shot which you refrained from playing would have been directed 'through' your opponent when travelling in a straight line to the front wall. If he decides 'clearly and undoubtedly' that this is so, he will award you a stroke.

So here's the moral. When you've played the ball, get out of the firing line. Get out of the triangle.

The third exception where a stroke may be awarded against a player who has made every effort to get out of his opponent's way is another fundamental squash principle. It is addressed to both players — not only the one who has just played the ball — and it confirms, if confirmation is needed, that squash is a 'no contact' sport.

- **If either player, at any time, makes unnecessary physical contact with his opponent the Referee may award a stroke against him.**

Now to summarize this very important rule (Rule 12) try to remember its name — 'Fair view, freedom to play the ball, and interference'.

Make every effort, otherwise you'll lose the stroke.

If you make *every* effort it will be a let, but remember:
a) you *lose* the stroke if your opponent could have
    played a winning shot;
b) you *lose* the stroke when your opponent has refrained
    from hitting you with the ball directly on its way to the
    front wall;
c) you *lose* the stroke if you make unnecessary physical
    contact with your opponent.

'Hitting an opponent with the ball'

If you're a novice, and you can't generate the sort of power which could do a lot of damage, you'll be excused for hitting your opponent on the bottom with a gently mis-hit shot.

But as you develop greater awareness of the rules and greater control of the ball you will, quite properly, be given much less sympathy if your opponents are found to be getting more than their fair share of ball bruises.

And why shouldn't you be ostracized? Why shouldn't you be sent into the dunce's corner? Squash is intended to be a non-contact sport and the rules have been carefully drawn up to protect the person who is losing points through the bad positioning or the bad sportsmanship of his opponent.

So operate within the rules and the spirit of the rules, and never expose yourself or your opponent to the risk of having an eye knocked out. Neither of you would enjoy it.

It is assumed when the phrase 'hitting your opponent with the ball' is used, that the ball would have made a good return after being struck. (This is irrelevant to a player who is hit by the ball after the third bounce.) Similarly, you should note that 'hitting an opponent' covers anything which the player is legitimately wearing or carrying. In other words, it includes hitting his racket or his clothing.

If a player is hit by the ball directly on its way to the front wall he loses the stroke. He should not have been in the triangle.

However, there's an exception. (There's always an exception!)

If a player is hit by the ball, directly on its way to the front wall after his opponent has turned on the ball to play it, or if, by allowing it to pass behind his body he has 'mentally turned', a let will be awarded — not a stroke.

But try not to turn. It isn't good squash.

In the majority of instances where a player is hit with the ball it shall be a let. Here are some typical examples:

- **Being hit by a ball which is going up, but towards a side wall.** (In other words, being hit by a properly played side-wall boast.)

- **Being hit by a ball which is going up after bouncing off a side wall.**

- **Being hit by a ball which is going up, but towards the back wall.**

- **Being hit by a ball which is going up after hitting the back wall.**

The last two examples, which involve back-wall shots, can be confusing and difficult for an experienced player to envisage. The back-wall boast is increasingly used by players as a recovery shot, so inevitably there will be situations where lets can be awarded when a player is hit by the ball on its way to — or from — the back wall.

To help digest all these rich facts here is a quick revision: if you're hit by the ball on its way to the front wall you lose the stroke, BUT if your opponent turned on the ball it's a let; everything else, if the ball's going up, warrants a let.

Don't rush away. There's one more exception.

The Referee will award a stroke to the striker of the ball if a winning shot has been intercepted.

You'd like an example? Try this one.

Try not to drop your racket!

'Play in a match to be continuous'

The rules of squash recognize and encourage the rewards which result from a player's persistence and superior fitness, so from the moment the first service is delivered, play must go on. In a squash court there is nowhere to hide — play must be continuous.

Of course intervals of one minute are permitted between games, and an interval of two minutes is allowed between the fourth and fifth games — if the match lasts that long.

During these intervals, players may leave the court provided they return and are ready to play at the end of the allotted time. If you're lucky enough to have a Marker he will use the phrase 'ten seconds' to call you back onto court or to prepare you for the start of the next game.

Bear in mind that a Referee can award a game, or a succession of games, to the opponent of a player who delays play by failing to get back on court, or, indeed, by using any persistent delaying tactics.

Special considerations should be brought to bear when the continuity of play is broken owing to injury.

If, through no fault of his opponent, a player is injured and delay arises, the injured player must either continue the match or concede it to his opponent.

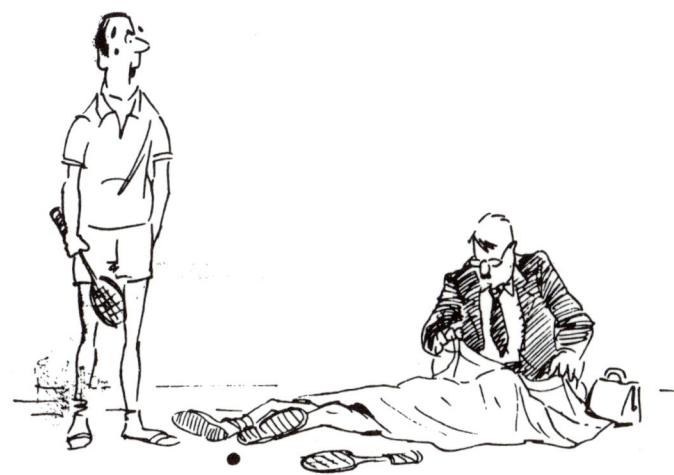

But where an opponent has 'contributed to' a player's injury, the injured person may be given treatment and allowed time to recover and resume play.

The extreme, and more serious, cause of delay resulting from injury arises when one person plays dangerously. Fortunately, the squash remedy is very simple indeed — the offending player will be asked to leave the court, and the match awarded to the injured player.

A disqualified player might feel the medicine of being asked to leave the court a bit strong, but he should remember that squash court injuries can be very, very serious, with far more at stake than the result of the match. Dangerous play will never be tolerated.

This brings us to other knotty and frequently misunderstood problems — those of obstruction, excessive swing, and injuries resulting from either.

Let us assume that it is your turn to play the ball. The rules are framed in such a way that you are entitled to delay your shot for as long as you like, provided you strike the ball before its second bounce on the floor.

Your opponent must make every effort to get out of your way although he won't always succeed because you might change your mind or perform an unexpected manoeuvre before you get to the ball.

Now we come to the important point. When you get to your chosen hitting area, you are standing in the centre of an imaginary circle. The circle represents the arc of a normal swing, and until you have struck the ball your opponent must stay out of your circle. If he is struck by your racket inside the circle he will be penalized for obstructing your legitimate stroke.

If he is struck by your racket inside the circle and is injured, it will be deemed to be a self-inflicted injury and he must continue playing, or concede the match.

All this assumes that the swing of the racket is normal, but occasionally a player's swing will not be normal. It will be excessive.

If you strike a player with an excessive swing outside your normal swing circle, you will be penalized. You risk disqualification if you injure your opponent.

Be careful.

The duties of the Marker

The Marker's principal function is to create a sense of peace and order in a boiling cauldron of physical activity and aggression.

Oh is that all?

As the person who calls out the score he is the principal communicator, and he will relieve the players and the Referee of many problems if he does his job efficiently — and sympathetically.

His terminology comes from a universally recognized squash language and it is particularly important, as a player, that you know the calls which are likely to be made by the Marker during a match.

Here are the calls, and their meanings:

Footfault Serving, without one foot being inside, and not on the line, of the service box.

Fault Serving into court, but incorrectly.

Out Serving the ball out of court, or hitting it out of court during a rally.

Not up Failing to return the ball above the board (or tin).

Down Hitting the ball onto the board (or tin).

It is important to remember that the Marker's decisions have to be made instantaneously, so mistakes will inevitably occur. Usually, without too much acrimony, the Referee will correct a Marker's incorrect call and play can be continued.

If a Marker is unsighted or uncertain about the legitimacy of a shot, he will say nothing until the end of the rally. Then, if necessary, he can obtain the Referee's judgement or, more likely, he will await the result of a player's appeal to the Referee.

When appropriate, the Marker should be particularly careful to call early and clearly, since players may infer that, by saying nothing, he has decided the ball was good and play should continue.

So if you're in the Marker's chair, be brave and make clear, early calls — especially service faults. A late call, or no call at all, can cause a player to rush a shot and lose a very valuable point.

And that's how Markers start losing friends!

The duties of the Referee

The Referee is the court of appeal. He awards 'lets' and 'strokes' and decides all appeals, including those against decisions made by the Marker. His word is absolute and final.

In a well-conducted match, the Referee's presence will hardly be noticed. He will be keeping the score and will only speak if one of the players makes an appeal, or if he decides to make a ruling without an appeal having been made by either player.

Generally, he will not interfere with the Marker's calling of the game unless he sees an error in the score or feels that a decision made by the Marker requires correction.

There are some circumstances in which the Referee has exceptional powers — life and death powers!

- **He may award the match to a player whose opponent fails to be present, on court, within ten minutes of the advertised time of play.**

However, commonsense normally prevails and if the reasons for the late arrival are sufficiently strong, the result of the match can be decided by the players on court, rather than by the Referee, off court.

- **He may stop play to warn the players about an infringement of the rules.**

This particularly applies where dangerous play is concerned or where the unreasonable conduct of one player is giving him an unfair advantage over his opponent.

- **He may order a player who has left the court to return and resume play.**

Players should not leave the court without first obtaining the Referee's permission unless, of course, they wish to leave for the normal intervals allowed between games.

After a proper warning has been ignored, the Referee can award a game to a player whose opponent has been employing delaying tactics. This includes hindering play by leaving court.

He can also award a game to the opponent of a player who has exceeded the timed interval between games.

But remember this — above all else:

- **In exceptional circumstances the Referee can, if he thinks fit, order a player to leave the court and then award the match to his opponent.**

It is difficult to imagine a wider power over life and death.

Fortunately, Referees are very rarely motivated to use their power of disqualification because their chief objective must always be the constructive one of helping players achieve a fair result.

In doing this a Referee will try to convey his decisions in a firm and precise manner, without imposing his personality on the match. Quite rightly, players are not amused when Referees talk to them like naughty children — it isn't necessary, and it invites problems especially when the Referee makes lousy decisions!

Unlike the Marker, who will try to make his calls as early as possible, the Referee must give deliberate and careful thought to every decision he makes. It is better to make a good decision late than a bad one early.

Have fun!

Squash players come in a multitude of shapes and sizes, but they all have one thing in common: they are highly intelligent, friendly people.

That's why, if you know the rules and can count up to nine, you can make good friendships wherever you go. Your awareness of the international code of conduct will make you a welcome member of the squash fraternity.

On the playing side, be prepared to meet wide variations in ability. Don't be afraid to accept help from other players, even if they are considerably better than you. The occasional thrashing won't do you any harm — it's all part of growing up.

But when you are good enough to hand out the occasional thrashing, try to do it with sympathy and understanding. That way, people will still talk to you when you're on the slippery slope downwards, and the game of squash will continue to benefit from your involvement.

The universal message for players, referees, markers and spectators alike is really very simple —

Squash rules. O.K.?

THE RULES OF THE SINGLES
GAME OF SQUASH RACKETS

Approved by the International Squash Rackets Federation (ISRF) to be effective from 1st May, 1980. (These rules refer to the game of Squash Rackets in respect of the game as played on courts, the specifications for which were first determined by The Squash Rackets Association (Great Britain).)

1. THE GAME, HOW PLAYED The game of Squash Rackets is played between 2 players with standard rackets, with balls officially approved by the ISRF and in a rectangular court of standard dimensions, enclosed on all 4 sides.

2. THE SCORE A match shall consist of the best of 3 or 5 games at the option of the promoters of the competition. Each game is 9 points up; that is to say, the player who first wins 9 points wins the game, except that, on the score being called 8 all for the first time, Hand-out may choose, before the next service is delivered, to continue the game to 10, in which case the player who first scores 2 more points wins the game. Hand-out must in either case clearly indicate his choice to the Marker, if any, and to his opponent.

— NOTE TO REFEREES —

If Hand-out does not make clear his choice before the next service, the Referee shall stop play and require him to do so.

3. POINTS, HOW SCORED Points can only be scored by Hand-in. When a player fails to serve or to make a good return in accordance with the rules, the opponent wins the stroke. When Hand-in wins a stroke, he scores a point; when Hand-out wins a stroke, he becomes Hand-in.

4. THE SERVICE
    (a) The right to serve is decided by the spin of a racket. Thereafter the server continues to serve until he loses a stroke, whereupon his opponent becomes the server, and so on throughout the match.
    (b) At the beginning of each game and each hand, the server has the choice of either box and shall thereafter alternate for as long as he scores points and remains Hand-in. However, if he serves a fault which is not taken, or a rally ends in a Let, he shall serve again from the same box. If the server serves from the wrong box, there shall be no penalty and the service shall count as if served from the correct box, except that Hand-out may, if he does not attempt to take the service, demand that it be served from the other box.
    (c) The ball, before being struck, shall be dropped or thrown in the air and shall not touch the walls or floor; it must be served direct on to the front wall between the cut line and the out of court line, so that on its return, unless volleyed, it falls to the floor within the back quarter of the court opposite to the server's box. Should a player, having dropped or thrown the ball in the air, make no attempt to strike it, it may be dropped or thrown again without penalty. A player with the use of only one arm may utilise his racket to propel the ball into the air before striking it.
    (d) A service is good when it is not a fault or does not result in the server serving his hand-out in accordance with Rule 4(f). If the server serves one fault, he shall serve again. Hand-out may take a fault, and if he attempts to do so, the service becomes good and the ball continues in play.

— NOTE TO REFEREES —

The receiver has not attempted to take a fault until he has clearly committed himself to playing the ball.

    (e) A service is a fault:
        (i) if at the time of striking the ball the server fails to have at least one foot in contact with the floor within the service box, and no part of that foot touching the line surrounding the service box (called a foot-fault).
        (ii) if the ball is served on to or below the cut line.
        (iii) if the ball first touches the floor on or outside the short or half court lines delimiting the back quarter of the court required in Rule 4(c).
        (iv) any combination of faults in the one service counts only as one fault.
    (f) The server serves his hand-out and loses the stroke:
        (i) if he serves 2 consecutive faults, excluding any that have been taken by Hand-out, when the ensuing rally has ended in a Let.
        (ii) if the ball touches the walls or floor before being struck or if he fails to strike the ball, or strikes it more than once.
        (iii) if the ball is served on to, or below, the board, or out, or against any part of the court before the front wall.
        (iv) if the ball, before it has bounced twice on the floor or has been struck by the opponent, touches the server or anything he wears or carries.

5. THE PLAY After a good service has been delivered, the players return the ball alternately until one or other fails to make a good return, or the ball otherwise ceases to be in play in accordance with the Rules.

6. GOOD RETURN A return is good if the ball, before it has bounced twice upon the floor, is returned by the striker on to the front wall above the board, without touching the floor or any part of the striker's body or clothing, provided the ball is not hit twice or out.

— NOTE TO REFEREES —

It shall not be considered a good return if the ball touches the board before or after it hits the front wall.

7. LET A Let is an undecided stroke, and the service or rally, in respect of which a Let is allowed, shall not count and the server shall serve again from the same box. A Let shall not annul a previous fault.

— NOTE TO REFEREES —

This last sentence applies only to a second or subsequent service after a fault has not been taken.

8. STROKES, HOW WON A player wins a stroke:
    (a) Under Rule 4(f);
    (b) If the opponent fails to make a good return of the ball in play;
    (c) If the ball in play touches his opponent or anything he wears or carries, except as is otherwise provided by Rules 9, 10 and 13(a) (i).
    (d) If a stroke is awarded by the Referee as provided for in the Rules.

9. HITTING AN OPPONENT WITH THE BALL If an otherwise good return of the ball has been made, but before reaching the front wall it hits the striker's opponent, or his racket, or anything he wears or carries, then:
    (a) If the ball would have made a good return, and would have struck the front wall without first touching any other wall, the striker shall win the stroke, except if the striker shall have followed the ball round, and so turned, or shall have allowed the ball to pass behind his body, in either case taking the ball on the forehand in the backhand side of the court or vice-versa, a Let shall be allowed.
    (b) If the ball would otherwise have made a good return, a Let shall be allowed unless, in the Referee's opinion, a winning stroke has been intercepted, then the striker shall win the stroke.
    (c) If the ball would not have made a good return, the striker shall lose the stroke. The ball shall cease to be in play, even if it subsequently goes up.

10. FURTHER ATTEMPTS TO HIT THE BALL If the striker strikes at, and misses the ball, he may make further attempts to return it. If, after being missed, the ball touches his opponent, or his racket, or anything he wears or carries, then:
    (a) If the striker would otherwise have made a good return, a Let shall be allowed;
    (b) If the striker could not have made a good return, he loses the stroke.
If any such further attempt is successful resulting in a good return being prevented from reaching the front wall by hitting the striker's opponent, or anything he wears or carries, a Let shall be allowed in all circumstances.

11. APPEALS
    (a) An appeal may be made against any decision of the Marker, except for (b) (i) below.
    (b) (i) no appeal shall be made in respect of the Marker's call of 'Foot-fault' or 'Fault' to the first service.
       (ii) if the Marker calls 'Foot-fault' or 'Fault' to the second service, the server may appeal, and if the decision is reversed, a Let shall be allowed.
       (iii) if the Marker allows the second service, Hand-out may appeal, either immediately, or at the end of the rally, if he has played the ball, and if the decision is reversed, Hand-in becomes Hand-out.
       (iv) if the Marker does not call 'Foot-fault' or 'Fault' to the first-service, Hand-out may appeal that the service was a foot-fault or fault, provided he makes no attempt to play the ball. If the Marker does not call 'Not up', 'Out', or 'Down' to the first service, Hand-out may appeal, either immediately or at the end of the rally, if he has played the ball. In either case, if the appeal is disallowed, Hand-out shall lose the stroke.
    (c) An appeal under Rule 6 shall be made at the end of the rally.
    (d) In all cases where a Let is desired, an appeal shall be made to the Referee with the words 'Let, please'. Play shall thereupon cease until the Referee has given his decision.
    (e) No appeal may be made after the delivery of a service for anything that occured before that service was delivered.

12. FAIR VIEW, FREEDOM TO PLAY THE BALL, AND INTERFERENCE
    (a) After playing a ball, a player must make every effort to get out of his opponent's way. That is:
       (i) a player must make every effort to give his opponent a fair view of the ball, so that he may sight it adequately for the purpose of playing it.
       (ii) a player must make every effort not to interfere with, or crowd, his opponent in the latter's attempt to get to, or play, the ball.
       (iii) a player must make every effort to allow his opponent, as far as the latter's position permits, freedom to play the ball directly to the front wall, or side walls near the front wall.

(b) If any such form of interference has occurred, and, in the opinion of the Referee, the player has not made every effort to avoid causing it, the Referee shall on appeal, or stopping play without waiting for an appeal, award the Stroke to his opponent.

(c) However, If Interference has occurred, but in the opinion of the Referee the player has made every effort to avoid causing it, the Referee shall on appeal, or stopping play without waiting for an appeal, award a Let, except that if his opponent is prevented from making a winning return by such interference or by distraction from the player, the Referee shall award the Stroke to the opponent.

(d) When, in the opinion of the Referee, a player refrains from playing the ball, which, if played, would clearly and undoubtedly have won the rally under the terms of Rule 9(a) or (b), he shall be awarded the Stroke.

(e) If either player makes unnecessary physical contact with his opponent the Referee may stop play and award a Stroke accordingly.

— NOTE TO REFEREES —

(i) The practice of impeding an opponent in his efforts to play the ball by crowding or obscuring his view is highly detrimental to the game. Unnecessary physical contact is also detrimental as well as being dangerous. Referees should have no hesitation in enforcing Rule 12(b) and 12(e) above.

(ii) The words 'interfere with' in Rule 12(a) (ii) must be interpreted to include the case of a player having to wait for an excessive swing of his opponent's racket.

13. LET, WHEN ALLOWED Notwithstanding anything contained in these Rules, and provided always that the striker could have made a good return:

(a) A Let may be allowed:
(i) if, owing to the position of the striker, his opponent is unable to avoid being touched by the ball before the return is made.

— NOTE TO REFEREES —

This Rule shall be construed to include the cases of the striker, whose position in front of his opponent makes it impossible for the latter to see the ball, or who shapes as if to play the ball and changes his mind at the last moment, preferring to take the ball off the back wall, the ball in either case hitting his opponent, who is between the striker and the back wall. This is not, however, to be taken as conflicting in any way with the Referee's duties under Rule 12.

(ii) if the ball in play touches any article lying in the court.

(iii) if the striker refrains from hitting the ball owing to a reasonable fear of injuring his opponent.

(iv) if the striker, in the act of playing the ball, touches his opponent.

(v) if the Referee is asked to decide an appeal and is unable to do so.

(vi) if a player drops his racket, calls out or in any other way distracts his opponent, and the Referee considers that such occurrence has caused the opponent to lose the stroke.

(b) A Let shall be allowed:
(i) if Hand-out is not ready, and does not attempt to take the service.

(ii) if the ball breaks during play.

(iii) if an otherwise good return has been made, but the ball goes out of court on its first bounce.

(iv) as provided for in Rules 9, 10, 11(b) (ii), 18 and 19.

(c) No Let shall be allowed when the player has made an attempt to play the ball except as provided for under Rules 10, 13(a) (iv), 13(b) (ii) and (iii).

(d) Unless an appeal is made by one of the players, no Let shall be allowed except where these rules definitely provide for a Let, namely, Rules 9(a), and (b), 10, 12, 13(b) (ii) and (iii).

14. NEW BALL At any time, when the ball is not in actual play, a new ball may be substituted by mutual consent of the players, or, on appeal by either player, at the discretion of the Referee.

15. KNOCK-UP

(a) Immediately preceding the start of play, the Referee shall allow on the court of play a period not exceeding 5 minutes to the 2 players together for the purpose of knocking-up, or in the event of a player electing to knock-up separately, the Referee shall allow the first player a period of 3½ minutes and to his opponent 2½ minutes. In the event of a separate knock-up, the choice of knocking-up first shall be decided by the spin of a racket. The Referee shall allow a further period for the players to warm the ball up if the match is being resumed after a considerable delay.

(b) Where a new ball has been substituted under Rules 13(b) (ii) or 14, the Referee shall allow the ball to be knocked-up to playing condition. Play shall resume on the direction of the Referee, or prior mutual consent of the players.

(c) Between games the ball shall remain on the floor of the court in view and knocking-up shall not be permitted except by mutual consent of the players.

16. PLAY IN A MATCH TO BE CONTINUOUS After the first service is delivered, play shall be continuous so far as is practical, provided that:

    (a) At any time play may be suspended owing to bad light or other circumstances beyond the control of the players, for such period as the Referee shall decide. In the event of play being suspended for the day, the match shall start afresh, unless both players agree to the contrary.

    (b) The Referee shall award a game to the opponent of any player who, in his opinion persists, after due warning, in delaying the play in order to recover his strength or wind, or for any other reason.

    (c) An interval of one minute shall be permitted between games and of two minutes between the fourth and fifth games of a 5-game match. A player may leave the court during such intervals, but shall be ready to resume play at the end of the stated time. When 10 seconds of the interval permitted between games are left, the Marker shall call 'Ten Seconds' to warn the players to be ready to resume play. Should either player fail to do so when required by the Referee, a game may be awarded to his opponent.

    (d) In the event of an injury, the Referee may require a player to continue play or concede the match, except where the injury is contributed to by his opponent, or where it was caused by dangerous play on the part of the opponent. In the former case, the Referee may allow time for the injured player to receive attention and recover, and in the latter, the injured player shall be awarded the match under Rule 19(d) (ii).

    (e) In the event of a ball breaking, a new ball may be knocked-up, as provided for in Rule 15(b).

— NOTE TO REFEREES —

    (i) In allowing for a player to receive attention and recover, the Referee should ensure that there is no conflict with the obligation of a player to comply with Rule 16(b), that is, that the effects of the injury are not exaggerated and used as an excuse to recover strength or wind.

    (ii) The Referee should not interpret the words 'contributed to by his opponent' to include the situation where the injury to the player is a result of that player occupying an unnecessarily close position to his opponent.

    (iii) The practice of serving faults deliberately in order to obtain an additional period of rest is contrary to the spirit of the game and Rule 16(b). When the Referee is satisfied that a player is doing so, he shall, after warning him, in terms of Rule 16(b) award the game to his opponent.

17. CONTROL OF A MATCH A Match is normally controlled by a Referee, assisted by a Marker. One person may be appointed to carry out the functions of both Referee and Marker. When a decision has been made by a Referee, he shall announce it to the players and the Marker shall repeat it with the subsequent score.

Up to one hour before the commencement of a match either player may request a Referee and/or a Marker other than appointed, and this request may be considered and a substitute appointed. Players are not permitted to request any such change after the commencement of a match, unless both agree to do so. In either case the decision as to whether an official is to be replaced or not must remain in the hands of the Tournament Referee, where applicable.

18. DUTIES OF MARKER

    (a) The Marker calls the play and the score, with the server's score first. He shall call 'Fault', 'Foot-fault', 'Not up', 'Out', or 'Down' as appropriate.

    (b) If in the course of play the Marker calls 'Not up', 'Out', or 'Down' or in the case of a second service, 'Fault', or 'Footfault', then the rally shall cease.

    (c) If the Marker's decision is reversed on appeal, a Let shall be allowed, except as provided for in Rules 11(b) (iii) and (iv) and 19(b) (iv) and (v).

    (d) Any service or return shall be considered good unless otherwise called.

    (e) After the server has served a fault, which has not been taken, the Marker shall repeat the score and add the words 'One fault', before the server serves again. This call should be repeated should subsequent rallies end in a Let, until the stroke is finally decided.

    (f) When no Referee is appointed, the Marker shall exercise all the powers of the Referee.

    (g) If the Marker is unsighted or uncertain, he shall call on the Referee to make the relevant decision; if the latter is unable to do so, a Let shall be allowed.

19. DUTIES OF REFEREE

    (a) The Referee shall award Lets and Strokes and make decisions where called for by the Rules, and shall decide all appeals, including those against the Marker's calls and decisions. The decision of the Referee shall be final.

    (b) He shall in no way intervene in the Marker's calling except:

        (i) upon appeal by one of the players.

        (ii) as provided for in Rule 12.

        (iii) when it is evident that the score has been incorrectly called, in which case he should draw the Marker's attention to the fact.

        (iv) when the Marker has failed to call the ball 'Not up', 'Out', or 'Down' and, on appeal, he rules that such was in fact the case, the stroke should be awarded accordingly.

(v) when the Marker has called 'Not up', 'Out', or 'Down' and; on appeal, he rules that this was not the case, a Let shall be allowed except that, if in the Referee's opinion, the Marker's call had interrupted an undoubted winning return, he shall award the stroke accordingly.

(vi) in exceptional circumstances when he is absolutely convinced that the Marker has made an obvious error in stopping play or allowing play to continue, he shall immediately rule accordingly.

(c) The Referee is responsible that all times laid down in the Rules are strictly adhered to.

(d) In exceptional cases, the Referee may order:
   (i) a player, who has left the court, to play on.
   (ii) a player to leave the court and to award the match to the opponent.
   (iii) a match to be awarded to a player whose opponent fails to be present on court within 10 minutes of the advertised time of play.
   (iv) play to be stopped in order to warn that the conduct of one or both of the players is leading to an infringement of the Rules. A Referee should avail himself of this Rule as early as possible when either player is showing a tendency to break the provisions of Rule 12.

(e) If after a warning a player continues to contravene Rule 15(c) the Referee shall award a game to the opponent.

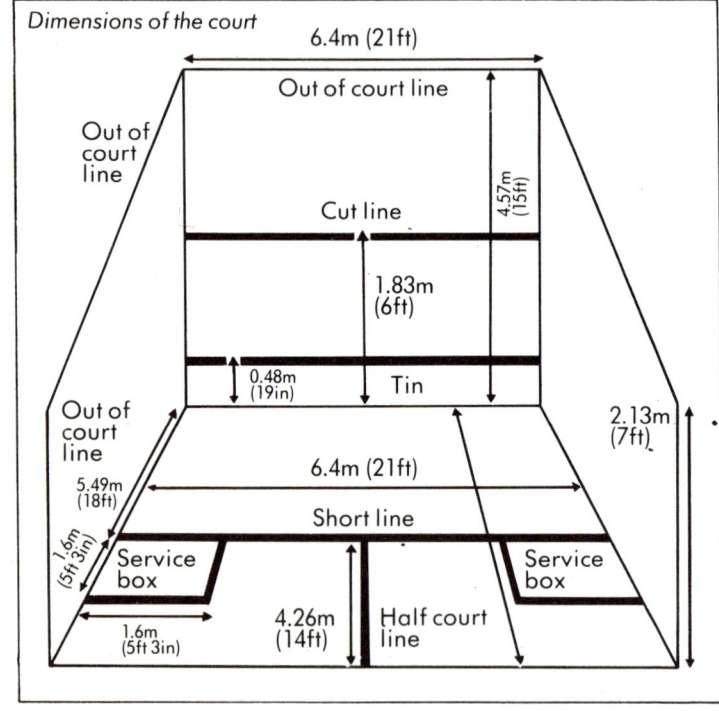

Dimensions of the court

6.4m (21ft) — Out of court line

Out of court line

4.57m (15ft)

Cut line

1.83m (6ft)

0.48m (19in) — Tin

Out of court line

2.13m (7ft)

5.49m (18ft)

6.4m (21ft)

Short line

1.6m (5ft 3in)

Service box — Service box

1.6m (5ft 3in)

4.26m (14ft)

Half court line

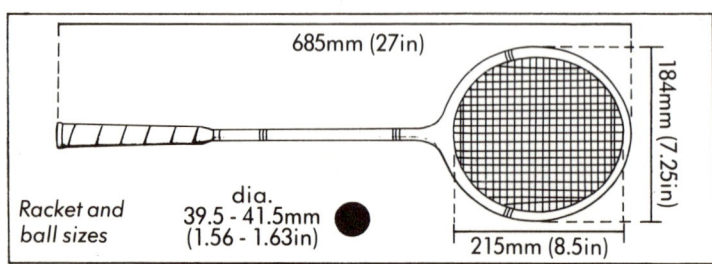

Racket and ball sizes

685mm (27in)

184mm (7.25in)

dia.
39.5 - 41.5mm
(1.56 - 1.63in)

215mm (8.5in)